AN ORACLE GUIDEBOOK

MOTIVATE ME!

WEEKLY GUIDANCE FOR HAPPINESS & WELLBEING

SHELLEY WILSON

ZANDER

Livonia, Michigan

Cover design, interior book design,
and eBook design by Blue Harvest Creative
www.blueharvestcreative.com

Cover border illustration by
Alli Kappen

Published by Zander
an imprint of BHC Press

Library of Congress Control Number:
2016959448

ISBN-13: 978-1-946006-25-7
ISBN-10: 1-946006-25-4

Visit the author at:
www.shelleywilsonauthor.co.uk &
www.bhcpress.com

Also available in eBook

ALSO BY
SHELLEY WILSON

NON-FICTION TITLES
How I Changed My Life in a Year
Meditation for Beginners
Vision Boards for Beginners

FICTION TITLES
Guardians of the Dead
Book 1 of The Guardians

Guardians of the Sky
Book 2 of The Guardians

Guardians of the Lost Lands
Book 3 of The Guardians

In Creeps The Night: An Anthology
Featuring "The House On The Hill"
by S.L. Wilson

INTRODUCTION TO THE
MOTIVATE ME! ORACLE GUIDEBOOK

Oracle books and cards have been a great comfort to me over the years. They helped me to move forward when I felt stuck, picked me up when I fell, and gave me an objective when I felt lost.

It's the powerful words and meanings that resonate, giving strength to commit to something, or deal with an issue that may be causing sleepless nights. We all seek answers to our whirling thoughts, and this guide-book aims to help you reach a conclusion.

Oracle books and cards come in all shapes and sizes, and in a huge variety of themes, from angels to the zodiac, cosmic ordering to goddesses or faeries. The themes may differ, but the messages are the same. They act as a guide to empower your daily life.

When I wrote the *Motivate Me!* book, I wanted to develop something that would help all year long; that is why I designed it with 52 pages. One for every week of the year.

HOW TO USE
THE MOTIVATE ME! ORACLE GUIDEBOOK

There is a variety of ways you can use this book. I've designed it to give you a weekly boost of inspiration. Choose one page every Monday morning as an affirmation and carry the book with you, or display it in your home or office. Remember to pick a new page every week.

Alternatively, it can be used for divination. Think of a specific question or issue, and when you feel ready, open the book at a random page. The answer will be there for you.

Although the oracle guidebook was designed for entertainment purposes, you do need to be willing to trust in its potential. When you are fully committed to finding an answer to a difficult issue, or just need advice, then this guidebook will help you.

AN ORACLE GUIDEBOOK

MOTIVATE ME!

WEEKLY GUIDANCE FOR HAPPINESS & WELLBEING

Just because things didn't go as planned
doesn't mean you failed.
Learn from everything you do,
make peace and move on.

Understand who you are.
You reap the best harvest
when you know where
your roots originate.

Variety is the spice of life.
Try and engage in something
new every day this week
and embrace the unfamiliar.
By learning to do this,
you will discover
how easy it becomes to spot
new opportunities.

What you wear
can lift your spirits.
Try and wear a brightly
coloured outfit
every day this week.
Notice the subtle differences
in your thoughts.

Include regular water breaks
in your day.
Allow yourself to achieve
a clearer mind.
Set an alarm on your phone
to go off every hour,
to remind you to rehydrate.

Write a list.
Note down your treasured friends
or favourite places to visit.
Rekindle your relationships by arranging
to meet your friends,
or visit these places.
Set a date to accomplish this and stick to it.

Release the fear you are holding on to.
FEAR is simply:
False Evidence Appearing Real.
You are safe to let it go.

Use this week to do something fun!
You are working too hard and need
to embrace your inner child.

Smile at a stranger.
Smile at your reflection.
Smile and be happy.
Smile.

You've been doing too much.
It's time to slow down.
Make a date with yourself this week
and recharge your energy levels.

Love what you do.
Engage 100% in your work/career.
If you can't, then maybe it's time to make a change.

To achieve your goals,
you need to enlist
support from your
family and friends.
Don't be afraid
to ask for help.

Make someone's day and
give them a compliment.
Learn to receive a
compliment in return.
'You are amazing.'

The time is right for you to
learn a new skill,
or to expand on your old skills.
When the student is ready, the
master will appear.

Pick a dream/goal that
is always on your mind
and brainstorm ways you
can make it happen.
Use a mind map to break
this goal into
bite-sized chunks and
find ways to begin
working towards its fruition.

Visit a place you've never been before.
It doesn't have to be far away;
it could be in your neighbourhood.
Embrace the new.

Book yourself a relaxing treatment,
such as a massage or a facial.
You deserve to look after
number one for a change.
You can't look after others
if you don't look after yourself.

Exercise is good for the
mind, body and soul.
Boost your energy levels by being
more active this week.

Write a list of everything
you are grateful for this week.
Refer to it often and add to it daily.
'I am grateful for…'

It's time to embrace your dreams.
Imagine what you want from life
and collect images to reinforce this.
Make a collage and look at it daily.

You are having doubts about
a situation or person close to you.
It's okay to change your mind.

Listen for the hidden
message to your question
in the song lyrics
you hear repeatedly.

Never give up hope.
Hold on to your dreams
and beliefs.
You are so close now.

The time isn't right
at the moment.
Wait a while; review your
thoughts and actions.
Come back to it later
in the year.

Do a selfless act
every day for one week.

Don't neglect your dreams.
Reaffirm your goals and take action.
Write a dreams list and keep it close.
Remind yourself daily of the reasons
you want to achieve this.

Even the most uncreative person
can benefit from art.
Take a timeout to doodle or colour in.
Use this as a meditation session.
Do this for five minutes,
once a week, or daily.

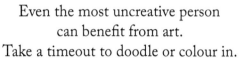

Find an inspirational mentor:
author, speaker, life coach or colleague.
Re-evaluate your goals.
What lessons can you learn from them?

You are not alone.
Make time this week to be
with your family and friends.
Reach out to them.

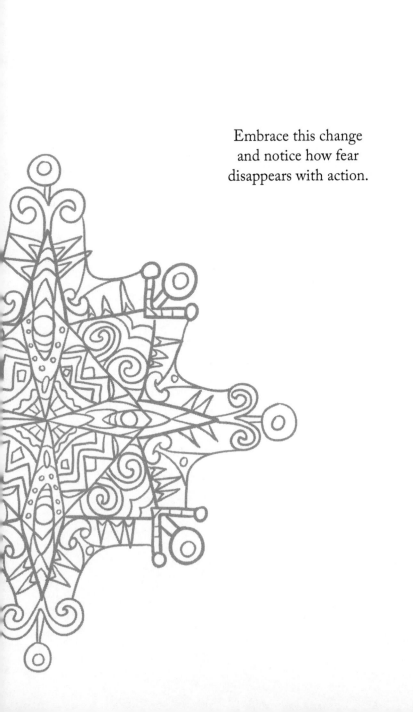

Embrace this change
and notice how fear
disappears with action.

Donate your time.
Someone needs you, and you know who it is.
Knowing they are supported will help
them to cope with a troubling situation
or emotional conflict.

We all suffer from self-doubt.
Understand that we can
learn just as much from
our failures as our successes.
Move on with your task
and free yourself from
this insecurity.
'Believe in yourself.'

Children laugh
four hundred times a day.
Adults laugh
four times a day.
Find the fun in your life
and learn to laugh more.

Focus on the experience,
not on the result.

Utilise a diary, calendar,
or app to streamline your life.
Be more organised this week.
Begin a new habit that
will allow more time for fun
and laughter, alongside
meetings, deadlines and
family/friend activities.

You don't have to struggle alone with this issue.
Ask for help and it will be given.

Take steps to declutter your
home or office this week.
By clearing your external environment,
you also cleanse internally.

Are you self-sabotaging?
Take time this week to purify
your mind and body.
Release negativity and
focus on the positive.

Streamline your life.
What changes can you make
this week to free up more time?

Challenges can be overcome
by sharing the load.
Ask for help.

Lose yourself in a make-believe world.
Pick a movie and embrace the big screen, or
choose an epic book and get lost in the pages.

Thoughts become things.
Focus on the positivity
in your life this week,
and bring more of
this energy to you.

Pick a positive affirmation,
one for each day of the week.
Jot them down and
carry them with you.
Live by them daily.

'I am happy.'
'I am abundant.'
'I am blessed.'
'I am grateful.'
'I am confident in my abilities.'
'I am in control.'
'I am healthy.'

People can become
overwhelmed by their lives.
Forgive them when
they exclude you, and
know that they still care.

Spend time this week
reconnecting with nature.
Find a place where you
can connect and recharge.
Take a walk during
your lunch break.
Potter in the garden.

It's okay to take a step back and regroup.
This allows for a new beginning.

Music feeds the soul.
Make a playlist of your favourite songs
and dance around the kitchen.

Your energy levels need a boost.
Look closely at what you are eating.
Fill your plate with fresh vegetables
and lean meat/fish.
Aim to eat colourful food this week.

Still your mind.
Use this week to meditate.
With a quiet mind, new opportunities
will show themselves,
and old problems will find a solution.

Take time out to read.
Choose a genre you
wouldn't normally pick.
Changing habits can
open up your mind.

What have you always wanted to do?
Take action towards doing it this week.
All great adventures begin with a single step.

If you know your goal,
then do some research on how to achieve it.
The time is right for you to act.

ABOUT
SHELLEY WILSON

Shelley Wilson divides her writing time between her young adult fantasy novels, and the motivational non-fiction titles she writes for adults.

Shelley lives in the West Midlands, UK with her three teenage children, an enormous goldfish and a black cat called Luna. She is at her happiest with a slice of pizza, a latte and *Game of Thrones* on the TV. She would love to live in the Shire but fears her five foot ten inch height may cause problems. She is an obsessive list writer, social media addict and full-time day dreamer.

You can check out all her books on Amazon:
www.amazon.co.uk/e/B00G5KPMJ1

Connect with the author:

www.shelleywilsonauthor.co.uk
www.facebook.com/FantasyAuthorSLWilson
www.twitter.com/ShelleyWilson72
www.instagram.com/authorslwilson

and at her publisher:
www.bhcpress.com

21190288R00037

Printed in Great Britain
by Amazon